THE TRUE STORY OF
Johnny Appleseed

Michigan

Goshen

Fort Wayne
1828
Mar. 18, 1845

St. Joseph River

Wabash River

St. Marys River

Maumee

Fort Wayne

Fort
Defiance
1828

St. Marys R.

Hancock Co.

St. Marys
Mercer Co.

Auglaize Co.

To Missouri 1843
and Iowa, probably
following watercourses

Fort Recovery

Logan Co.

Greenville

1826
Urbana
Champaign

N
W — E
S

Richmond

Clark Co.

Old Town

Legend

Buffalo & Indian Trails ......
Indian Towns ▲
J. A's nurseries 🌳
and dates
J. A's cabins 🏠
Memorials ✳
📖

Indiana

The Gore

Treaty Line 1795

← 500 miles →

Oxford

Great Miami River

Little Miami R.

Fort Hamilton

Mad River

Virginia Military Lands

Shawnee Trail

Zanes Trace

1826
Cincinnati
Fort Washington

Miami Purchase

To the Mississippi River

Big Bone
Lick

Kentucky

River

Iroquois War Path

To New Orleans

Limestone

Map drawn by Florence Murdock 1945

THE TRUE STORY OF
Johnny Appleseed

Ophia D. Smith

CHRYSALIS BOOKS
WEST CHESTER, PENNSYLVANIA

This essay originally appeared in 1945, "Centennial Tribute," The Swedenborg Press, Patterson, N. J.; second edition, 1946; third edition, 1947; fourth edition, "Memorial Highway Edition," 1953; fifth edition, 1957; sixth edition, 1966, Johnny Appleseed Memorial Library, Cincinnati, Ohio; and was reprinted in *Johnny Appleseed: A Voice in the Wilderness*, edited by William Ellery Jones (West Chester, Pa.: Chrysalis Books, 2000).

Acknowledgment: The publisher wishes to thank Mr. Joseph W. Smith, son of the late Ophia D. Smith, for his permission to reprint this essay.

Library of Congress Cataloging-in-Publication Data

Smith, Ophia D. (Ophia Delilah), b. 1891.
The True story of Johnny Appleseed / Ophia D. Smith.
     p. cm.
ISBN-13: 978-0-87785-323-7
  1. Appleseed, Johnny, 1774–1845. 2. Apple growers—United States—Biography. 3. Frontier and pioneer life—Middle West. I. Title.

SB63.C46S65 2007
634'.11092—dc22
[B]   2006035205

Designed and typeset by Karen Connor
Printed in Canada
All Rights Reserved in "Johnny Appleseed" stamp image ©United States Postal Service. Used with Permission.

Chrysalis Books is an imprint of the Swedenborg Foundation, Inc. For more information, contact:
    Chrysalis Books
    Swedenborg Foundation
    320 North Church Street
    West Chester, PA 19380
    or
    http://www.swedenborg.com.

About *the* Author

OPHIA D. SMITH (1891-1994) was initially a piano teacher. At the age of forty, during a slow recovery from a near-fatal illness, she became interested in history. Among her friends were Swedenborgians, intelligent, thoughtful women, who may have inspired Mrs. Smith to study the early Swedenborg Church in Ohio, resulting not only in "The Story of Johnny Appleseed," but a series of scholarly articles on the New Jerusalem Church and early churchmen for the *Ohio State Archeological and Historical Quarterly*. Subsequently, she wrote, with her husband William E. Smith, former chairman of the Department of History at Miami University in Ohio, a biography of Col. John H. James, founder of Urbana University.

Ophia D. Smith's work is carried on by the Smith Library of Regional History in Oxford, Ohio, opened in 1981 and named for Dr. and Mrs. Smith.

The people of old Spain had a maxim that whoever eats a fruit must plant the seed; otherwise, he is ungrateful to the past and unjust to the coming generation. Whenever a Spaniard ate a fruit, he dug a hole in the ground with his toe, placed the seed therein, and scraped a bit of earth over it with his foot. As a consequence, there was an abundance of fruit in Spain to be had for the taking, along highways and in remote places. The Spaniard who should be credited with this practical idea has been forgotten, but the name of the man who did more than any other to plant orchards in the old northwest is widely known. His parents gave him the name of John Chapman; those who loved him for his kindly deeds called him "Johnny Appleseed."

For fifty years, this rugged old pioneer toiled along the water-courses and wilderness trails to provide apple trees for the immigrants who came west, and to spread the doctrines of Emanuel Swedenborg.* Even his name possesses a certain significance, for "John" literally means "Jehovah hath been gracious," and "Chapman" means an itinerant merchant who, in colonial days, carried chapbooks of a religious nature among his wares. Johnny Appleseed was a chapman who carried Swedenborgian tracts and books to give away to anyone who would read them.

---

* Emanuel Swedenborg (1688–1772) was an eighteenth-century theologian and mystic whose writings are the basis for the Church of the New Jerusalem or New Church.

As those who knew him passed from earthly to spiritual life, Johnny became a legendary figure; and although some of his friends and acquaintances wrote down their recollections of him and the work he did, these stories, "begot in the ventricle of memory" and written "upon the mellowing of occasion," now frequently confound the researcher. To separate truth from fancy often is well-nigh impossible.

Only recently has the ancestry of John Chapman been established. It is now known that John was a direct descendant of Edward Chapman, who came from Yorkshire, England, to Boston in the 1640s and became a prosperous farmer and miller in Ipswich. John was of the sixth generation from Edward. He was the second child of Elizabeth Simonds and Nathaniel Chapman who were married at Leominster, Massachusetts, on February 8, 1770. John was born at Leominster on September 26, 1774, and was baptized with his sister Elizabeth in the Congregational Church on June 25, 1775, the day his father and mother were received into that church. John's father, Nathaniel, was a carpenter, a farmer, and a

Revolutionary War soldier. So far as any records show, he was a man of little means, though there is a tradition that he lost two good farms in the service of his country.

A letter from Elizabeth to Nathaniel, dated June 3, 1776, suggests that she was suffering from an advanced case of tuberculosis. At that time, Nathaniel was with a company of carpenters attached to General Washington's headquarters at

New York. In this letter, Elizabeth stated that she had money for her needs, although she had not bought a cow, for cows were scarce and dear. This was a time of hardship and war-time inflation when many a colonial mother had a hard time caring for her children.

On June 26, 1776, Elizabeth gave birth to her third child, a son. On July 18, she died, and within two weeks, according to family tradition, the baby, too, was dead. Little John, not yet two years old, and his sister Elizabeth were cared for, presumably, by kind relatives. After Elizabeth's death, Nathaniel continued to serve in the Continental Army.

In the summer of 1780, Nathaniel Chapman, captain of wheelwrights under Major Eayres, was honorably discharged from the army.[1] In the summer, he was married to Lucy Cooley of Longmeadow, Massachusetts. To them were born ten children.*

Whether Elizabeth's children went to live with Nathaniel and Lucy or not, John sustained intimate relations with the family. According to family tradition, John, at the age of eighteen, persuaded his half-brother Nathaniel, a lad of eleven, to go west with him. This was in 1792.[†]

Since the deeply worn "Connecticut Path" from Boston to Albany crossed the Connecticut River at Springfield, one may presume that the boys saw emigrants passing to the West every day and that they constantly heard glowing stories of that wonderful land. For almost half a century, New Englanders had turned longing eyes toward the Susquehanna. They had first heard of it from missionaries returned in their efforts to convert the Native Americans to the Christian faith. These stories spread throughout Connecticut and Massachusetts by word of mouth and through the press.

---

* Florence E. Wheeler, "John Chapman's Line of Descent from Edward Chapman of Ipswich," *Ohio State Archaeological and Historical Quarterly* XLVIII, 21, 39–41; Robert Price, "The New England Origins of Johnny Appleseed," *New England Quarterly* XII, 454–469.

† Anna Long Onstott, *New Church Messenger*, Sept. 30, 1942.

Little companies of emigrants were organized, and they set out for the fabulous country two hundred miles away, crossing the Hudson River at about where the present town of Catskill stands. This was just half way to the Susquehanna. Under the most favorable conditions, it took two or three weeks of the hardest kind of travel and labor to reach the headwaters of the Susquehanna.*

John Chapman is said to have been in the Wilkes-Barre region some time in the 1790s,[2] practicing his profession as a nurseryman;† just when he embraced the Swedenborgian faith and began his missionary activities we cannot be sure, although it is probable that it was before he ever reached western Pennsylvania.[3] Two or three writers who knew Johnny Appleseed say that he sometimes spoke of his activities as "a Bible Missionary" on the Potomac when he was a young man. One writer claims that Johnny was seen for two or three successive years along the banks of the Potomac in eastern Virginia, picking the seeds from the pumice of the cider mills, in the late 1790s.‡

---

* Anna Long Onstott, *New Church Messenger*, Sept. 30, 1942.

† Price, "A Boyhood for Johnny Appleseed," *New England Quarterly* XVII, 393; W. M. Glines, *Johnny Appleseed by One Who Knew* Him (Columbus, Ohio: 1922).

‡ Geo. Wm. Hill, *History of Ashland County* (Ashland, Ohio: 1880), 184.

From the Potomac, he could have worked his way westward to Fort Cumberland. From Fort Cumberland, he could have followed Nemacolin's Path, better known as Braddock's Road, to the Monongahela, and followed the Monongahela to Pittsburgh, a route that many New Englanders took because there were fewer Native Americans to be encountered along the southern route.

When Johnny was only ten years old (1784), George Washington traveled this road to survey the possibilities of the West. On that trip, he saw the "fingertips of the Potomac" reaching toward the Youghiogheny and the Monongahela, and caught the vision of canals and portage roads to join the Hudson, the Susquehanna, the Potomac, and the James. John Chapman, too, caught a vision of the future development of the West as he traversed the wilderness. It is said that he procured his seeds from the settlers along the Monongahela to plant his nurseries at Braddock's Field, at Wheeling, on the Grave Creek Flats, at Holliday's Cove, and that he returned there for seeds.*

---

* General Roeliff Brinkerhoff, Scrapbook, Clipping No. 21, a letter from S. C. Coffinberry to editor of the Mansfield, Ohio, *Shield and Banner*, dated Constantine, Michigan, Nov. 23, 1871. The Brinkerhoff Scrapbook is in the Library, Ohio State Arch. and Hist. Museum, Columbus, Ohio.

From Pittsburgh, according to one story, the Chapman boys went up the Allegheny River to its confluence with Olean Creek at Olean, New York. They expected to find an uncle there, but he had moved on. The boys appropriated the cabin and stayed through the winter, suffering much hardship. The next year, they again took up their nomadic life in western Pennsylvania until their father, with his large family, went west in 1805.* Presumably, the Chapmans lived at Marietta while the boys cleared a farm on Duck Creek. Nathaniel, senior, had plenty of manpower in his family to clear and plant and build. The fertile soil of the Muskingum Valley offered a marked contrast to the stony fields of Massachusetts.

Johnny, however, went up and down the Muskingum and its tributaries planting his apple seeds from the Monongahela. By instinct, he practiced the Van Mons theory of improving fruit by seeding rather than by grafting or budding.† He was not unique in that he planted seedling nurseries. Many early nurserymen planted seeds, but they did not itinerate as he did. In 1790, Ebenezer Zane had an extensive seedling nursery in Zanesville. There were some small orchards, of course, planted by the Native Americans from the seeds of the fine orchards of the French traders and missionaries.

---

* Price, "A Boyhood for Johnny Appleseed," 392.
† *Ohio Cultivator*, Sept. 1, 1846.

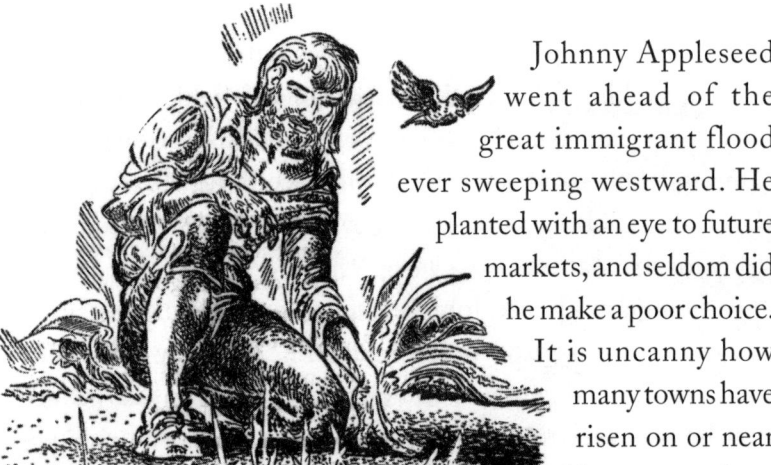

Johnny Appleseed went ahead of the great immigrant flood ever sweeping westward. He planted with an eye to future markets, and seldom did he make a poor choice. It is uncanny how many towns have risen on or near his nursery sites. Had he used that native shrewdness to make money for himself, he might have been considered a man of substance, rather than an eccentric old man who planted apple seeds; but then he would never have become the subject of song and story and the object of veneration that he is today.

John Chapman appeared on Licking Creek, in what is now Licking County, Ohio, in 1800, when he was twenty-six years old. He had probably come up the Muskingum River to plant near the Refugee Tract, which would soon fill up with settlers, when Congress actually got around to granting the lands. In April 1798, the Continental Congress had ratified resolutions to donate public lands for the benefit of those who had left Canada and Nova Scotia to fight against the British in the Revolutionary War. The lands were actually set apart in 1801 and patents issued in 1802. Grants of land ranging from 160 acres to 2,240 acres were awarded according to the exertions of the patentee in the war. Johnny, with true Yankee enterprise, went ahead and planted his nurseries before the refugees arrived. Licking County, then a part of Fairfield, contained only three caucasian families. When William Stanberry came, in 1809, to settle near the confluence of the Muskingum River and Licking Creek, Johnny Appleseed's trees were ready for the market.

At Stanberry's house, Johnny often spent the night, usually sleeping out in a grove near the house. Stanberry said that Johnny ate only vegetables. Some of Johnny's friends have said that he was very fond of milk and honey, because he considered them heavenly foods.

Chapman was always eager to make converts to the New Church. It seemed to be his "main business" to "leave the books wherever he could get anybody to read them." Johnny was always delighted to find a family that was eager for something to read. One of the books that Johnny carried with him was Swedenborg's *Heaven and Hell*. As the Stanberrys and Johnny read together Swedenborg's description of hell, they agreed that it described accurately the town of Newark. At that time, Newark was largely given over to horse-racing and hard liquor.

Johnny was thoroughly familiar with his Bible and the writings of Swedenborg. There was nothing he liked better than a theological argument. He could present his

thesis with cogency and penetration. To him, the Swedenborgian idea of the future life was amazingly simple. He said once to William Stanberry's brother, "It is no more mysterious to me or even to you that you should live in different zones after death than that you live in them now." When asked by John Vandorn of Richland County what he would do for a living in the next world, he replied, "Well, I will follow the same occupation as I do here, but with more pleasure and happiness."*

Johnny Appleseed must have been one of the earliest Swedenborgians in America. The first General Convention of the New Jerusalem in the United States of America met in Philadelphia in May 1817. Four months prior to the Convention, a report of Johnny's labors was published in Manchester, England. At the Fifth General Convention, also held in Philadelphia, Johnny Appleseed's missionary work was again reported at some length. In a letter dated Philadelphia, May 15, 1821, Daniel Thunn wrote to Margaret Bailey at Cincinnati:

* N.N. Hill, *History of Licking County* (Newark, Ohio, 1881), 239–240; Joshua Antrim, *History of Champaign and Logan Counties from Their First Settlement* (Bellefontaine, 1872), 149–153; F. B. Pearson and J. D. Harlor, *Ohio History Sketches* (Columbus, 1903), 52; Henry Howe, *Historical Collections of Ohio* (2 vols., Cincinnati, 1904), II, 69; Letter, written by John H. James, Jan. 23, 1857, from Urbana, Ohio, to the Cincinnati Horticultural Society; Brinkerhoff Scrapbook, Clipping No. 20.

. . . To add something more to the New Church news, there is Mr. John Chapman near Wooster, Ohio, who wrote lately to Mr. Schlatter that he found an increase of Receivers all around his neighborhood and that they are spreading as far as Detroit, he proposed to make a Deed over to the New Church for a Quarter Section of Land and take payment in Books of the New Church. We contemplate how best to fulfill his wishes. This is the Appleseed man you certainly must have heard of, who goes around in the Country to plant Apple Trees.

This letter seems to bear out the tradition that Johnny Appleseed had nurseries planted around Richmond, Indiana, when the first settlers arrived. Already, in 1804, a few families were pushing into "the gore" along the Whitewater River in Indiana Territory. The Greenville Treaty Line (1795) established a boundary that ran from Lake Erie by way of the Cuyahoga and Tuscarawas Rivers westward to Fort Recovery (Greenville, Ohio) and southwestward to the Ohio, opposite the mouth of the Kentucky River, thus forming a gore-shaped tract on the Indian side of the Ohio state line. At least one Methodist preacher settled on Elkhorn Creek

near the present town of Richmond in 1805. By 1808, a circuit rider was covering Indiana Territory as far north as Richmond and westward across Indiana and Illinois Territories, and across the Mississippi River into Missouri.*

If the Methodists found enough settlers to warrant so much activity, there was undoubtedly a market for apple trees. In his role as a precursor of the frontier, Johnny could have come to Cincinnati down the Ohio a few miles, and up the Whitewater into the vicinity of Richmond. It is claimed that the earliest settlers around Richmond knew Johnny Appleseed and that he stopped in their cabins.

According to W. M. Glines, who knew the Chapman family, Johnny Appleseed planted a nursery on the school lands at Delaware, Ohio; made a small improvement there; and went on to Sandusky. He might have followed the Warrior's Path (Cumberland Gap-Sandusky) which was the shortest way between Delaware and Sandusky and a route likely to be traveled by immigrants. From Sandusky, he could

---

* Helen V. Austin, "Johnny Appleseed, the Pioneer Pomologist of the West," *Indiana Horticultural Society Transactions* XXII, 35–40, reprinted in *Missouri State Horticultural Society Annual Report* XXXIII, 13–18; Wm. C. Smith, *Indiana Miscellany* (Cincinnati, 1867), 49–51; *History of Wayne County, Indiana* (2 vols., Chicago, 1884), I, 355; "Johnny Appleseed, a Pioneer Benefactor" in 1840–1940 series in Richmond (Ind.) *Palladium*, 1940.

have followed the Sandusky-Pittsburgh Trail to the Forks of the Mohican. In this region, Johnny made his headquarters for some time. That he had several nurseries on the Mohican is evident from an order written by him: "Due John Oliver one hundred and fifty trees when he goes for them to some of my nurseries on Mohecin waters."*

Johnny Appleseed was seen in 1806, floating down the Ohio River with two canoes lashed together and filled with apple seeds. Upon landing at Steubenville, he announced that he had come to plant his seeds. He planted his first nursery in Jefferson County not far from Steubenville at what is now the town of Brilliant. This was a logical place for a nursery, for under the Harrison Land Law of 1800, Steubenville was one of the four Ohio land offices, where a

settler could buy land at two dollars an acre, making a down payment of only fifty cents an acre.†

John Chapman came into the Firelands with the first settlers, or what was already there, in 1811. The Firelands, a tract of land that constitutes Huron County, was granted by Connecticut (1792) to certain citizens of that state whose homes had been burned or otherwise laid

* E. O. Randall, ed., "'Johnny Appleseed' Addendum," *Ohio State Arch. and Hist. Pub.* (Columbus, 1901), IX, 315.

† W. H. Hunter, "The Pathfinders of Jefferson County," *Ohio State Arch. and Hist. Pub.*, VI, 291; Dana Elbert Clark, *The West in American History* (New York, 1937), 248.

waste in the Revolutionary War. Caleb Palmer, a surveyor, came into the Firelands in 1810 and returned with a man named Woodcock in 1811, just two years after Huron County was formed. Johnny Appleseed made his home at Palmer's for some time and was intimately associated with Palmer and Woodcock.*

Johnny Appleseed had the satisfaction of seeing the last tree from his Firelands nurseries set out, and some of his neighbors had to go to one of his nurseries in Delaware County to secure apple trees for planting.† Johnny helped these hardy pioneers with their work, as he went among them telling about his apple trees and of "the good news right fresh from Heaven." Some writers say that he was a cranberry peddler. Thousands of bushels of cranberries were harvested from the marshes of the Firelands by squatters and sold to remote settlers. Cranberries, huckleberries, "shack pork," wild meat, coonskins, and produce from small potato patches constituted most of the frontier currency.‡ Wherever Johnny Appleseed went, he paid his own way.

He had unusual ideas about charging for his trees and collecting for them. He would take a reasonable price in money, some cast-off clothing, a

---

* A. G. Stewart, "Memoirs of Townships. New Haven," *Firelands Pioneer* I, 9; Mrs. H. J. Heller, "New Haven," *Firelands Pioneer* XV, 1081.

† "Greenfield in 1819," *Firelands Pioneer* XI, 89.

‡ Heller, "New Haven," 1074.

bit of food, or nothing at all, according to the circumstances of his customer. To him, it was more important for a settler to plant a tree than to pay for it. He never liked to have a note dated for a specific day; for, said he, it might not be convenient to collect that day, or it might not be convenient for the customer to pay on that date. He never asked a man to pay a debt, for he reasoned that, if God wanted him to have the money, God would move the customer to pay. Besides, the customer knew that he owed the money, without being reminded of it.

C hapman was methodical in the selection of his nursery sites and the planting of his seeds. He always selected a good loamy piece of ground in an open place, fenced it in with fallen trees and logs, bushes, and vines; sowed his seeds; and returned at regular intervals to repair the fence, to tend the ground, and to sell his trees. If he had to remain long with a nursery, he put up a little Indian hut of poles and covered it with a bark roof, leaving a hole in the center for the smoke to escape. His housekeeping equipment consisted of a camp kettle, a plate, and a spoon. He sometimes made a bed of leaves inside the hut, but often he slept on the bare ground with his feet to a small fire. Sometimes he slept on a bed of leaves beside a log; again, he might make himself a temporary shelter by leaning great slabs of elm bark against a fallen tree; inside, on his bed of leaves, he slept serenely, confident that nothing could harm him. Men came from long distances to buy trees from him and then stayed the night. With his meager equipment, Johnny boiled mush and dispensed hospitality as graciously as any housewife.*

When Johnny put out a large nursery, he sometimes erected a small log cabin for his use, inviting a husky neighbor or two to assist him. Two of the Vandorn boys of the Lexington (Richland County) neighborhood went into the forest to help him raise a cabin some time after the close of the War of 1812. They arrived one evening about dusk. Johnny was standing close to a fire kindled by the side of a large log. He was very glad to see them. There he was, four miles from a living soul, among catamounts, wolves, bears, snakes, and porcupines, yet happy and content. Five or six rods from the fire were logs already cut for a cabin and some clapboards for the roof. After sitting down and talking for a while, Johnny poked in the ashes with a stick and pulled out some roasted potatoes. From under the log he pulled a bag of salt. This simple fare he offered his guests, saying, "This is the way I live in the wilderness." He went on to say, "I could not enjoy myself better anywhere. I can lie on my back, look up at the stars, and it seems almost as though I

* Hill, *History of Ashland County*, 183–187.

can see the angels praising
God, for he has made all
things for good." One of
the boys opened their sack
of provisions and laid out
on some clapboards bread
and butter and dried ven-
ison, inviting Johnny to
share it. Johnny ate some of their bread and butter, and they ate
some of Johnny's baked potatoes and salt.

After the meal had been eaten, Johnny entertained the boys
with stories about the Seymours and the Dutchman Ruffner.
He said that the settlers were to blame for all the mischief
the Native Americans had done. He had always found the
indigenous tribes friendly and kind. He told the boys about
two natives who came to his camp to tell him of a forest fire
and helped him to keep it away from his camp and his nursery.

Before going to bed, the boys moved a log and discovered a
rattlesnake, shaking its rattles and ready to
strike. The boys wanted to kill it, but Johnny
would not allow it, saying that the Native
Americans did not kill snakes. He went on
talking until the boys were sleepy. Then they
lay down upon some clapboards, with
their heads under Johnny's bark shed and
their feet to the fire. The howling of the
wolves startled the boys, and up they jumped with their guns,
but Johnny said, "Tut, tut, lie down and go to sleep. I like to

hear them howl." Just as the boys were again dozing off, an owl hooted. In an instant, one of the boys sprang up, gun in hand, yelling, "Indians! Indians!" Johnny only said, "Do let me sleep. I like to hear the owls hoot." He drew up his feet, turned over on his log, and in a moment was peacefully snoring.*

In the Mohican country, Johnny visited every cabin religiously, feeling that he had been commissioned to preach, to heal diseases, to warn of danger—in short, he helped God take care of the settlers. He planted his nurseries around Mansfield, Loudonville, Perrysville, and the Indian village of Green Town, living in a little cabin near Perrysville. When asked why he feared neither man nor beast, he replied that he lived in harmony with all people, and that he could not be harmed as long as he lived by the law of love. He is said to have sown the seeds of medicinal herbs wherever he went—dog fennel, pennyroyal, catnip, hoarhound, mullein, rattlesnake root, and others. For a long time, fennel was called "Johnny weed." The idea that he sowed these seeds may have come from the fact that he used them in concocting simple remedies for common ailments. He sometimes appeared at the door of a new settler's cabin with a gift of herbs in his hand.

---

* Brinkerhoff, *Scrapbook*, Clipping no. 20.

When Johnny came to the Mohican country, Native Americans greatly outnumbered the new settlers. Mansfield contained only two or three cabins, and its two blockhouses were not built until the late summer of 1812. There was a blockhouse at Beam's Mill on Rocky Fork, a picketed house belonging to Thomas Coulter on Black Fork, and a blockhouse where Ganges now stands. All supplies had to be brought in by packhorse from Mount Vernon in Knox County. It is said that when Benjamin Butler came to lay out the town of Mount Vernon in 1805, he found Johnny Appleseed already there.

Among the native tribes in this region were Delawares and Wyandots. There was a settlement of Delawares at Jerome's Town and one at Green Town, a village of sixty cabins and a large bark council house. There was also an Indian village nearby called Hell Town. Other Native American towns were Mohegan John's Town, Beaverhat's Town, White Woman's Town (on the Walhonding), Killbuck's Town, and Coshocton, the Delaware capital. A number of Indian trails passed through this region, the main one being the south branch of the old Fort Duquesne-Sandusky-Detroit Trail.* These natives were friendly with the settlers from the time of the signing of the Treaty of Greenville in 1795 to the outbreak of the War of 1812. The Native Americans who stirred up the trouble in

---

* I. M. Heyde, *A Brief Centennial History of Loudonville*, 6, 7.

the beginning of that war were Tecumseh and his brother, the Prophet.*

Johnny made friends with the Native Americans and spoke their language. They looked upon him with a sort of superstitious awe and considered him a great medicine man. His unusual zeal for serving others led the indigenous tribes to believe him touched by the Great Spirit. For that reason, they allowed him to listen to their council meetings, and he was therefore sometimes able to avert trouble between the Native Americans and the settlers. Completely free of race consciousness, he understood the viewpoint of both races.

TECUMTHA.

Johnny Appleseed could read the book of Nature as readily as any Native American, and he could clothe his thoughts in language as vividly pictorial as that of any orator. Johnny could understand the symbolism of their religious rites and their ideas of a future life, for he, too, thought in pictures.

During the War of 1812, Johnny Appleseed was ever on the lookout for trouble with the Native Americans. One of the earliest settlers of the Firelands, Hanson Read, made arrangements with Johnny to come to his house

---

* James F. M'Gaw, *Philip Seymour or Pioneer Life in Richland County Founded on Facts* (Mansfield, 1858), 5–6, 22-23, 46, 112.

once a week to let him know how things were going in the war. One day in the late summer, Read was out in the woods hunting his cows, when Johnny suddenly appeared in the clearing, shouting, "Fly for your lives, the Canadians and Indians are landing at Huron!"

The Reads packed up immediately, hid their iron ware and some of their most valuable things in the woods, took Mrs. Read and her young baby with some bedding and other necessities on a sled and started for the blockhouse at Mansfield.

Johnny continued on, stopping at every cabin door to warn of danger. However, it turned out that the British and the Indians were not coming, after all. Johnny had seen a large number of General Hull's soldiers, who had been captured and robbed of their clothing and arms, landing at Huron. They had been sent back by the British in a destitute condition, each soldier wrapped in a blanket provided by his captors.

The Reads lived in one of the blockhouses until January, Mr. Read working in a brickyard. One night he failed to return at the usual time. The people became much alarmed, and a report came in that Read had been scalped. After a while, Read came in unharmed, to tell that a man named Jones, a storekeeper, had been murdered a short distance from town. The villagers fled to the blockhouses, and Johnny Appleseed volunteered to go to Mount Vernon, twenty-six miles away, for help. Johnny ran through the night, over a new-cut road, stopping at each lonely cabin to warn against the attacks.[4] When he reached Mount Vernon, Captain William Douglas mustered as many of his men as he could and left orders for the rest to follow. He took up the line of march about three o'clock in the morning and reached Mansfield about ten o'clock with

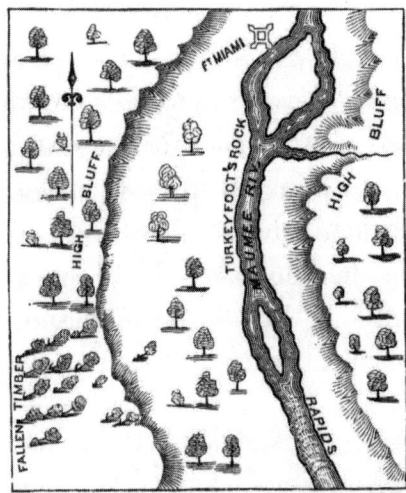

Johnny and the troops. When Johnny was asked how he accomplished the feat of bringing help so quickly, he replied that God gives the strength for the appointed task.*

After the excitement of the war had died down, Johnny Appleseed worked his way over into the Maumee Valley. A treaty was made at the foot of the Maumee Rapids, in 1817, by which a large tract of land in the Maumee Valley was ceded to the United States. The land was but a wilderness, with no improvements other than those made by the Native Americans. As the tribes removed westward, settlers appropriated the deserted cabins and lived in them until they could make their own improvements. Many settlers lived in an Indian hut

---

* Frank D. Read, "Pioneer Life in Huron County," *Firelands Pioneer* V, 126; Col. Edward Wheeler, "Firelands Reminiscences," *Firelands Pioneer* II, 37; M'Gaw, *Philip Seymour*, 108; A. J. Baughman, "Johnny Appleseed," *Ohio State Arch. and Hist. Pub.*, IX 309.

when they first came to the new lands
in Ohio and lived as primitively
as did Johnny Appleseed.
The "New Purchase" was
slow to attract settlers, but
Johnny went ahead to plant
for the market that would
surely develop.

Johnny Appleseed was often seen around St. Mary's. He stayed all night with the family of Samuel Scott on their "Old Town" farm west of St. Mary's, on an average of twice a year. Scott said that, in winter, Johnny wore cast-off shoes, tied on with many-colored strings wound around his ankles in all directions, but that in summer he went barefoot. He sometimes wore one shoe only, breaking the snow with the shod foot. He was known in the Maumee Valley as something of a philosopher, a Swedenborgian, and a dispenser of books. Once a year, he came through to see about his nurseries, continuing on his way to inspect his apple trees on the Auglaize and the Maumee, all the way to Lake Erie.[*]

He started a nursery about one mile above Defiance about 1828, at the mouth of the Tiffin River. Defiance was then a town only six years old. It had been an important trading post between the Canadian French and Native Americans. Johnny planted a nursery of several thousand trees, taking up later to reset on a more favorable

---

[*] Wm. F. McMurray, *History of Auglaize County, Ohio* (2 vols., Indianapolis, 1923), I, 535.

tract of land. There they remained until a resident agent sold them out. Most of the early orchards on the Maumee and Auglaize bottoms in Defiance, Paulding, and Henry Counties are said to have been started from Johnny's nursery near Defiance.*

Local records show and traditions indicate that John Chapman had nurseries in Ashland, Auglaize, Champaign, Coshocton, Clark, Crawford, Defiance, Delaware, Guernsey, Hancock, Huron, Jefferson, Knox, Licking, and Logan Counties. The construction of the Miami Canal was recommended in 1824, and it was actually begun in Middletown, Ohio, in 1825. It would have been a natural procedure, on Johnny's part, to plant nurseries all along the proposed route of the canal to Toledo. Other counties that claim Johnny Appleseed nurseries are Butler, Carroll, Harrison, Mercer, and Warren.

Johnny Appleseed occasionally visited Swedenborgian families in Cincinnati, in Hamilton County. Among these families was the Eckstein family. Mrs. Jane Eckstein was the daughter of Francis Bailey of Philadelphia who was the first publisher of Swedenborg's works in America and the first New Churchman in America.

---

* *History of Defiance County, Ohio* (Chicago, 1883), 109–110; J. D. Simkins, *Early History of Auglaize County* (St. Mary's, 1901), 70–71; Howe, *Collections*, 539, 541–542. For pioneer life of this region, see H. S. Knapp, *History of the Maumee Valley* (Toledo, 1872).

Bailey died in 1817, and his widow with a son and three daughters removed to Cincinnati the next year. Jane Bailey Eckstein and her husband came to Cincinnati a few years later to take charge of the school established by the Misses Bailey.

Francis Bailey's youngest daughter, Abbe, married John H. James of Cincinnati, and the young couple removed to Urbana, Ohio, to make their home. In 1826, Alexander Kinmont, a New Churchman who had married Mrs. James's niece, sent John Chapman to John H. James for legal advice concerning a nursery in Champaign County. Johnny Appleseed had planted the nursery with the permission of a certain landholder. Now that the land had been sold, he wanted to know if the new owner could dispossess him of his trees. He did not seem particularly anxious about the trees, however. He walked to and fro as he talked, eating nuts all the time. James invited him to go home with him to meet his wife and her sister Miss Bailey, but he modestly declined, feeling that he was not properly attired to meet the daughters of Francis Bailey.

New Church records show that Johnny Appleseed had traveled as far north as Detroit by 1821. According to an old document found in the Mercer County courthouse, John Chapman went out to Fort Wayne, Indiana, to make his home in 1828, after he had established his nurseries along the Maumee and the Auglaize. One autumn day in 1830, a citizen of Fort Wayne saw him seated in a section of a hollow tree loaded with apple seeds fresh from the cider presses of the Maumee settlements, landing at Wayne's Fort at the foot of Main Street. The seeds were wet from washing them free of pumice, and the improvised boat was covered with mud and tree moss.*

It is said that Johnny planted nurseries at the headwaters of the Illinois River in Grundy County, and New Church records show that he was in Illinois in the 1830s. At that time, there was a revival of land sales in that state. After the Land Law of 1820, it was possible to secure an eighty-acre farm for $100 in cash. It seems entirely possible that Johnny might have followed the portage paths from the Maumee to the Kankakee River to establish nurseries in the new lands then being sold to prospective settlers.

That Chapman made a trip to Iowa in the fall of 1843 is stated by Silas Mitchell, who at that time was living in Whiteside County, Illinois. Johnny passed through Whiteside

---

* *Indiana Historical Bulletin* XII, 76; Ft. Wayne Johnny Appleseed Memorial Commission booklet.

County on foot and stopped at the home of
a friend to stay all night. He said that he had
been to Iowa and that he was on his way to
Philadelphia to a New Church convention.*
After the close of the Black Hawk War, the
fifty-mile strip known as the Black Hawk
Purchase was quickly settled. By the
time that Johnny Appleseed went
there, the Native
American title to
the lands had been
extinguished, releasing
to settlement the fertile Des
Moines Valley, and immigrants were swarming into the Purchase and into the native lands beyond the legal boundary.†
Chapman is said to have gone into southern Michigan to
Holland, Cassopolis, and St. Joseph.

In the Midwest, there are many stories of Johnny Appleseed. Johnny always takes on the trappings of the local folk
hero, and often becomes attached to some local event of
importance. In Kentucky, they will tell you that he knew
Abraham Lincoln and John James Audubon, and that his
sweetheart died in Owensboro on the eve of their wedding. In
Missouri, they will tell you that he married an native girl, and
that he warned a French refugee against the indigenous tribes,
saying

---

* A. Banning Norton, *A History of Knox County, Ohio* (Columbus, 1962), 50. This must
have been in the fall of 1842, for the General Convention met in Philadelphia in June 1843.
  † Clark, 187–188.

The Story *of* Johnny Appleseed

I sow while others reap
Be sure my warnings keep
Indians will come by break of day
*Indians hunting scalps, I say.**

In Missouri folklore, he is a fiddler and singer of ballads. He may have sung ballads, but it is hard to imagine him carrying a fiddle in a bag that could have held apple seeds and the writings of Swedenborg. It is equally difficult to think of him singing in a public square and taking alms from a fortuitous audience.

From Johnny's contemporaries, we are able to gain some idea of his personal appearance. He is described as small and wiry, of average height, quick in speech, and restless in motion. His cheeks were hollow and his body spare because he walked so much and ate so little. His face and neck were bronzed and lined by wind and sun. He had extraordinarily brilliant eyes, dark and piercing. He had a well-shaped head and wore his long, black hair parted in the middle and tucked behind his ears to fall about his neck and shoulders. His hair was fine and glossy. A coal-black beard, lightly set and carelessly groomed, gave him a somewhat vagabond look. He never used a razor but sometimes trimmed his beard with a pair of scissors. He was not handsome, surely, but there was something compelling in those deep-set burning eyes.

---

* Iantha Castlio, "A Folk Tale of Johnny Appleseed," *Missouri Historical Review* XIX, 622–629.

He possessed a peculiar eloquence, too. He could hold an apple in his hand and discourse so charmingly upon that fruit that it became a thing of exquisite beauty and delight. He is said to have had a resonant voice that could be persuasively tender, inspirationally sublime, or witheringly denunciatory. He possessed a keen sense of humor, quick to make a witty retort or a cutting rebuke. He was sincerely patriotic, too. He had unlimited faith in his country. On one occasion, at least, he made a Fourth of July oration—at a celebration in the cabin of Levi Cole in Huron County.*

Johnny may not have been well-dressed, even by frontier standards. He is pictured as wearing a buttonless shirt, open to wind and sun and rain and snow, bloused over to form a pocket for his Bible. His trousers were short and frazzled at the bottom from briars and burrs, and were supported in a half-hearted fashion by some original substitute for suspenders. Much has been written about the tow-linen coffee sack he wore for a coat and the tin pot he wore upon his head. The latter would be simply a matter of efficiency. To one who

---

* Martin Kellogg, *Norwalk Reflector*, June 25, 1883.

had to sustain life and earn a living with what he carried upon his back, it was only natural to make one thing take the place of two. Obviously, he could not make mush in a hat or cap. Sometimes he wore a crownless hat, which, if he chose, he could carry on his arm. Again, he might be seen wearing an old revolutionary soldier's hat, sometimes with tracts snugly anchored beneath its crown. In short, he wore on his head whatever was convenient. As for the tow-linen coat, with a hole cut for his head, that was not so unusual. Many a circuit-rider cut a hole in a blanket, pulled it over his head, and wore it for a coat. Fastidious theater-goers of early Cincinnati complained because gentlemen from Kentucky attended the play in blankets rather than coats. Salathiel Coffinberry, who knew Johnny well, said that Johnny's coat was not a coffee sack, that it was "a kind of long-tailed coat of tow-linen then much worn by farmers." Johnny designed the coat himself. It consisted of one width of the coarse fabric, which reached from his shoulders to his heels. Coffinberry's mother made it for Johnny under his immediate supervision, cutting the two armholes and setting in a pair of straight sleeves.*

Aside from the scantiness of his attire, Johnny dressed much as other men in the more remote settlements. Both men and women went barefooted in summer, although they wore moccasins or shoe packs in winter to keep out the cold. It was said that he could walk over the ice and snow barefooted in the

---

* Brinkerhoff Scrapbook, Clipping No. 22.

coldest weather and never feel it. The skin was so thick on his feet that one of his acquaintances said it would kill a rattlesnake to try to bite Johnny's feet. He was peculiarly insensitive to pain. He could sear a wound with a red-hot poker and never flinch. He learned from the Indians to sear a wound and treat it as a burn. The common dress of the frontiersman in 1800 was a pair of dressed deerskin or blue cloth pantaloons, a blue handkerchief tied over the head, deerskin moccasins on the feet, and a blanket coat tied round the waist with a belt. From one side of the belt was suspended a pouch of dressed polecat skin to hold tobacco, pipe, flint, and steel. Under the belt on the other side a butcher knife was carried.* A blue linsey hunting shirt with a belt fringed in gay colors was considered very fine. In summer, farmers wore long-tailed tow-linen shirts, something like a peasant's smock. As to poverty of purse, Johnny probably had more money in his pocket than many a settler, and more than most itinerant preachers, who received from twenty-eight to one hundred dollars a year.

As for Johnny's diet, it was a little more frugal than that of many of the pioneer Methodist circuit-riders. They carried jerked meat and journey bread

---

* *History of Wayne County, Indiana,* I, 369.

for their food. Johnny ate nuts and fruits in their season, made mush in his tin pot, or ate sparingly of a bit of food given him by some generous housewife. He would not eat meat because he thought it wrong to destroy life. Johnny must have carried journey bread at times. That was a standard traveling food among the Native Americans. It was so highly nutritious and portable that the soldiers in the War of 1812 were advised to carry it with them on their marches. Notices were published in the newspapers with full directions for its preparation. It was made by boiling green corn in the roasting ear until half done, drying it in the sun for a few days, browning it in hot ashes, pounding it fine, and finally mixing it with maple sugar.

In his pack, Johnny sometimes carried a present of tea for some housewife who needed a bit of cheer, although he never drank tea himself. He carried a piece of bright calico or a gay ribbon for a child who had saved apple seeds for him during

the winter. Children never laughed at Johnny Appleseed. He was their friend. He could tell the most engaging stories; he could whistle and sing the gayest tunes; he could care for a childish hurt in the tenderest way. The little folk trotted at his heels and helped to plant his seeds or care for his young seedlings. As they worked together, Johnny told them of the beautiful land of the New

Jerusalem, dropping seeds of truth into young and tender hearts that bore fruit in after years. He told them of the glorious future of the brave new nation they must help to build—a land of opportunity for all. Johnny helped the men with their work and told the news from other settlements. One farmer said that Johnny was the best hand to shuck corn he ever had. Another said that Johnny could split as many rails and girdle as many trees in one day as most men did in two. Johnny was no beggar.

A round Fort Wayne, John Chapman bought up tracts of land amounting to 214 ½ acres in Allen and Jay Counties. There are traditions that he owned land in Mount Vernon, Mansfield, and the present town of Lakefork in Ohio, at various times, before he went to Indiana.[5] For many years, Johnny planted and tended his nurseries along the main highways—the rivers and the canals. On the north bank of the Maumee River in Milan Township, he owned a nurs- ery of fifteen-thousand apple trees. He became a familiar figure on the streets of Fort Wayne. In his later years, when strength was failing, he walked beside an old gray horse that he hitched to a cart to draw his load of trees or seeds.* Johnny never rode a horse. He would not allow it to do for him what he could do for himself. In the Mohican country, he had been noted for his tenderness toward mistreated and worn-out horses. He bought them up and arranged for their care until he could find good homes for them. He was never known to sell a horse.

Johnny's half-sister, Persis Chapman Broome, lived near Fort Wayne, and it is thought that he lived with or near her at times.[6] Her husband helped him with his nurseries. It was near the home of Persis Broome that Johnny apparently intended to make a permanent home. On this tract in Jay County, he had a nursery of two-thousand trees. On it, at the time of his death, there was already a log cabin, timber dressed and cut for a barn, and eleven acres cleared and fenced. The improvement on the land was done by William Broome.†

In 1842, Johnny made his last trip back to Ohio. While there, he made his headquarters at the home of Nathaniel, the brother who had accompanied him to Pennsylvania so long ago. Upon his return to Fort Wayne, he resumed his work as "a gatherer and planter of apple-seeds." On March 18, 1845, he died of pneumonia in the home of his old Richland

---

* Robert C. Harris, *Lawn Care*, Feb., 1935.

† Estate Papers of John Chapman, Allen County, Indiana.

County friend, William Worth. At the sawmill of Christian Parker, a plain walnut coffin was made for Johnny, and he was buried by his friends in a burial plot not far from Fort Wayne.*

The place of Johnny Appleseed's burial is a controversial subject. Some claim that he was buried in David Archer's graveyard, and others say that he was buried on the Roebuck farm. According to a letter written by Dr. T. N. M'Gaw to Judge Brinkeroff, Richard Worth told M'Gaw:

> *We buried him respectably in David Archer's graveyard two and a half miles north of Fort Wayne, he having died at my father's house which to him was a comfortable and welcome home in his old age.*†

John Chapman lived in complete harmony with nature. In field and meadow and forest he walked, concerned with the spacious thoughts of God. In his earthly life, he was a one-man circulating library, a one-man humane society, a one-man clinic, a one-man missionary band, and a one-man emigrant-aid society. Johnny Appleseed did not need to die to find heaven, for heaven was in his heart.

---

* *Fort Wayne Sentinel*, March 22, 1845; Rosa A. Langtry, "A Visit to the Grave of Johnny Appleseed," *Indiana History Bulletin* IV, 218–220; Wesley S. Roebuck, "Outline of Facts Related to the Burial Place of John Chapman," *Ohio Arch. and Hist.* Quar. LII, 275–284. See Price, "References to Death, Burial Place and Estate" in *John Chapman: A Bibliography of "Johnny Appleseed" in American History, Literature and Folklore* (Patterson, N.J.: Swedenborg Press, 1944), 11–13.

† See letter in Brinkerhoff Scrapbook, Clipping No. 20. The letter is dated Norristown, Indiana, June 13, 1858.

Endnote Updates by William Ellery Jones

1. In Robert Price's later book *Johnny Appleseed, Man and Myth*, he states on page 16 that John's father, Nathaniel, along with other Springfield officers, was released in late 1780 because of "unsatisfactory management of the company stores." It appears now, however, that Price misinterpreted what limited records were available to him at the time and that Chapman's father had been exonerated.

In an unpublished manuscript, "Let's Put the Record Straight," which was an offshoot of formal documentation prepared for and filed with the Massachusetts Society of the Cincinnati, George B. Huff, FACG, has cleared his ancestor Nathaniel Chapman's name. The following is excerpted with permission by Mr. Huff:

> *The Springfield Armory came into existence as General Washington and his staff felt the urgent need for an additional artillery regiment in 1776. . . . Major Joseph Eayre was ordered to command a company of Artillery Artificers at Springfield in January 1777. . . . Nathaniel Chapman, on March 19, 1777, was assigned as Captain of Wheelwrights at Springfield, pursuant to appropriate action by Colonel Henry Knox and/or a warrant of the Board of War, where he remained until September 30, 1780. Perhaps as a reward for good service or perhaps to clarify his commissioned status with the Massachusetts troops, Congress, on 7 May 1778, passed a Resolve, "That the Board of War having recommended Nathaniel Chapman, Esq. to be captain of the additional company to*

Colonel Flower's regiment of Artillery artificers." The successful conduct of the war where it began in the north had by the Fall of 1779 moved the scene of combat to the south which made a marked effect on the efficiency of the Springfield operation to transport their manufactured, refurbished and restored equipment to the combat troops so far away in the south. This had an interesting effect on their entire supply system for the type of munitions Springfield produced that caused the Board of War to consider "derangement" or demobilization as a practical method of closing down the Springfield post. The Journals of the Congress, Volume XVII, 1780, show concerns for the lessening utility of the armory and began a reduction in force by excusing a number of personnel from further service at that post. Later, on August 26, 1780, Congress passed a Resolve, "That Major Joseph Eayre and Captain Nathaniel Chapman, who have been employed at Springfield in the department of the Commissary-General of the military stores; be excused from further service." The Board of War went further to report that Captain Chapman (and others) be entitled to one year's pay and subsistence.

2. Traditions based on recollections of Judge Lansing Wetmore, an early chronicler of Warren County, Pennsylvania, have John and perhaps his half-brother Nathaniel arriving near Warren in the middle of an early November 1797 snowstorm. The earliest known written record of John Chapman's having been in Pennsylvania is found in John Daniel's store ledger. It was discovered in the early 1950s and contains six entries on page 39 regarding Chapman's purchases in Warren, interpreted by some to have begun on February 14, 1797, and ended on May 3, 1799. Further, six other entries on page 121 include what are believed to be his half-brother Nathaniel's transactions, from June 26 to November 12, 1798.

3. The earliest known reference to Chapman's having possibly been introduced to the Swedenborgian faith is reported in Carl Theophilus Odhner's *Annals of the New Church* (Bryn Athyn, Pa.: 1904). New Church tradition claims Chapman's first contact was through Judge John Young, while in Greensburg, Westmoreland County, Pennsylvania, although this association has not been proved. Young, a close member of Francis Bailey's Swedenborg reading circle in Philadelphia, moved his law practice to Greensburg in 1790, where he continued to introduce the doctrines and distribute Swedenborg publications.

4. *The Ohio Register*, Clinton, Ohio, August 10, 1813, was first to report Johnny Appleseed's run:

> *Tuesday Evening, 10th Inst. An express arrived at this place from Mansfield, which place he had left at sunset— stated that the Indians had attacked that Town killed and scalped a Mr. Jones—several men were missing. A number of mounted men from Clinton and vicinity [Mount Vernon] have gone to their assistance.*

Now, for the first time, confirmation of this incident and its date can be set with confidence. Witnesses to the affair identified Chapman as the messenger and one claimed, "It was the brightest moon that night I ever saw." Lunar tables have been checked and, indeed, the night of August 9–10, 1813, enjoyed a full moon. Once again, it seems that the right man for the job was available at the right time and that the hand of Providence illuminated the way.

At the time of Johnny's run, Mansfield's Square was the site of two blockhouses erected during the War of 1812 and very few other structures. One blockhouse, constructed of round logs by a Captain Schaeffer of Fairfield County, Ohio, stood at the intersection of Main and Park Avenue West. Colonel Charles Williams of Coshocton County, Ohio, built the other blockhouse of hewn logs. It was located in the middle of the north side of the square and soon served as Mansfield's first courthouse. The settlements of Clinton and Mount Vernon, Ohio, were in close proximity to each other and located about twenty-six miles south of Mansfield.

5. These traditions have been confirmed in land records of Richland and Ashland Counties, as have others in Ohio counties. His first known recorded property consisted of two town lots in Mount Vernon, Ohio, which he purchased for $50 on September 14, 1809 (Knox County Deeds A, 116). It has been estimated that Chapman likely held deeds to almost 1,200 acres of land at various times throughout his lifetime.

6. According to early records of Green Township, Ashland County, Ohio, Persis and William Broom lived near Perrysville from about 1816 to 1830 and just west of Mansfield, Ohio, on the old Leesville Road (500 West Fourth Street) from about 1830 to 1835, after which it is believed they moved to Jay County, Indiana.